Colors

Blue

by Sarah L. Schuette

Reading Consultant:
Elena Bodrova, Ph.D., Senior Consultant,
Mid-continent Research for Education and Learning

an imprint of Capstone Press
Mankato, Minnesota

A+ Books are published by Capstone Press
151 Good Counsel Drive, P.O. Box 669, Mankato, Minnesota 56002
http://www.capstone-press.com

1 2 3 4 5 6 07 06 05 04 03 02

Library of Congress Cataloging-in-Publication Data
Schuette, Sarah L., 1976–
    Blue / by Sarah L. Schuette.
    p. cm. — (Colors)
    Summary: Simple text and photographs describe common things that are blue, including blueberries, bluebirds, and blue jeans.
    Includes bibliographical references and index.
    ISBN 0-7368-1467-1 (hardcover)
    1. Blue—Juvenile literature. [1. Blue.] I. Title.
QC495.5 .S362 2003
535.6—dc21   2002000702

Created by the A+ Team
Sarah L. Schuette, editor; Heather Kindseth, production designer; Patrick D. Dentinger, production designer; Gary Sundermeyer, photographer; Nancy White, photo stylist

The A+ Team thanks Michael Dahl for editorial assistance.

Note to Parents, Teachers, and Librarians
The Colors series uses full-color photographs and a nonfiction format to introduce children to the world of color. *Blue* is designed to be read aloud to a pre-reader or to be read independently by an early reader. Photographs and activities help early readers and listeners understand the text and concepts discussed. The book encourages further learning by including the following sections: Table of Contents, Words to Know, Read More, Internet Sites, and Index. Early readers may need assistance using these features.

Table of Contents

Blue is cloudy and
blue is bright.

Blue is the largest whale in sight.

The blue whale is the largest animal living on Earth. Whales swim in the blue ocean.

7

Blue is juicy.
Blue is round.

Blueberries are blue fruits that grow on shrubs. Blueberries taste good on top of pancakes or cereal.

Blue poison dart frogs
live in the rain forest.
Blue frogs jump and hop
to get to where they
are going quickly.

Blue can hop across the ground.

Bluebirds are songbirds
with bright blue feathers.
Female bluebirds lay
blue eggs.

Blue has feathers and blue sings.

More Blue

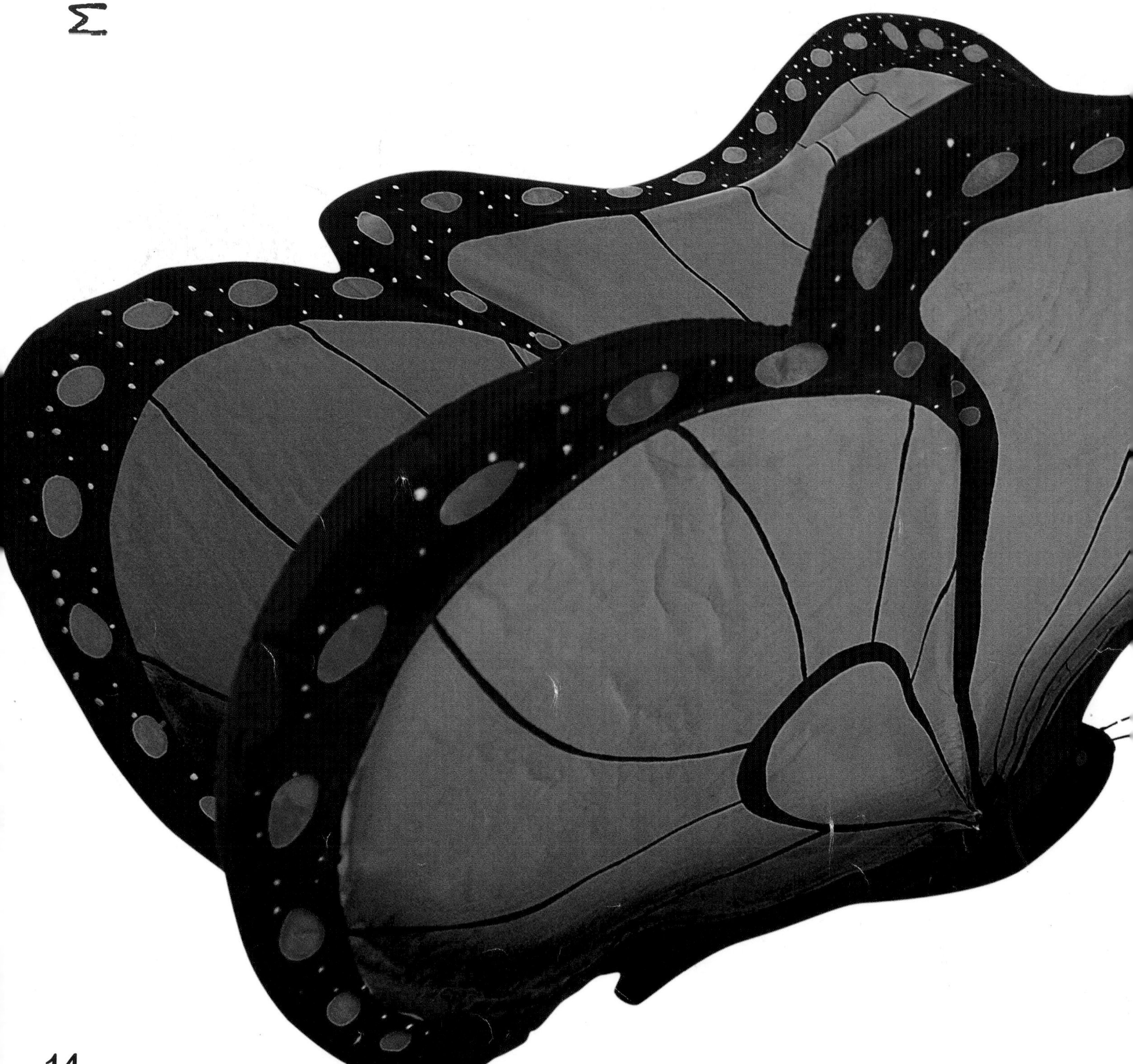

The Western Pygmy Blue is one of the smallest butterflies in the world. It has a wingspan the same size as a pencil eraser.

Blue flutters with four blue wings.

Blue can say you
won first place.

A blue ribbon stands for a first place prize. Science fairs and races give blue ribbons to winners.

Blue protects your head and face.

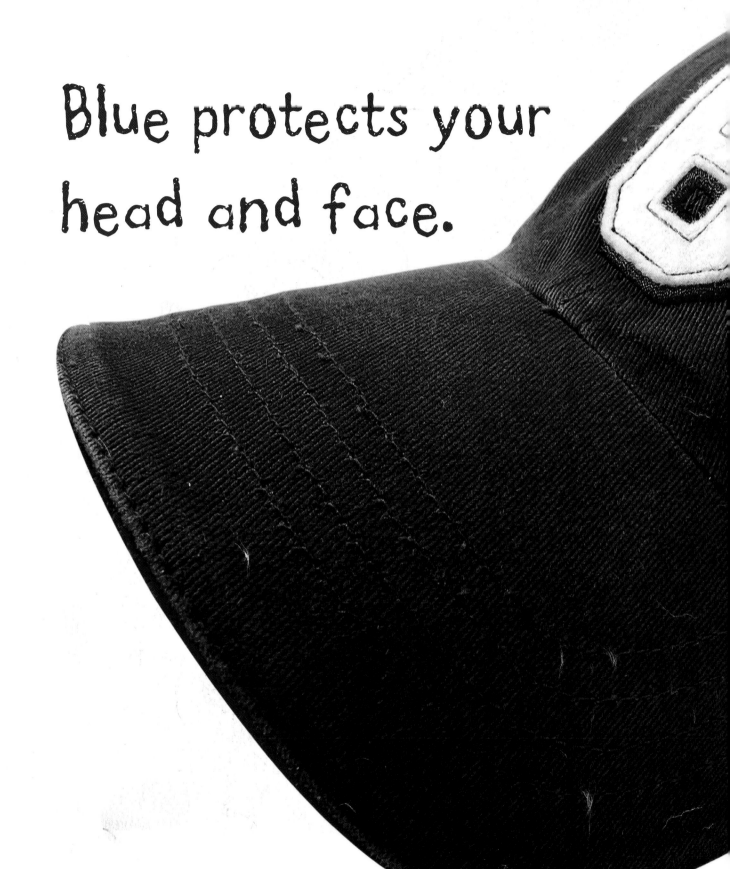

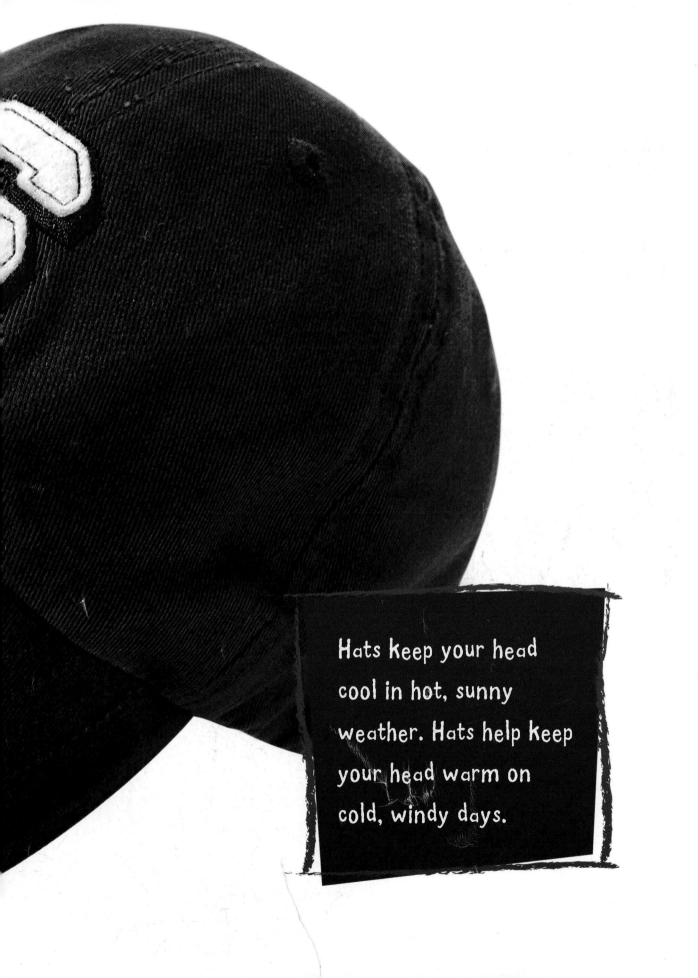

Hats keep your head cool in hot, sunny weather. Hats help keep your head warm on cold, windy days.

19

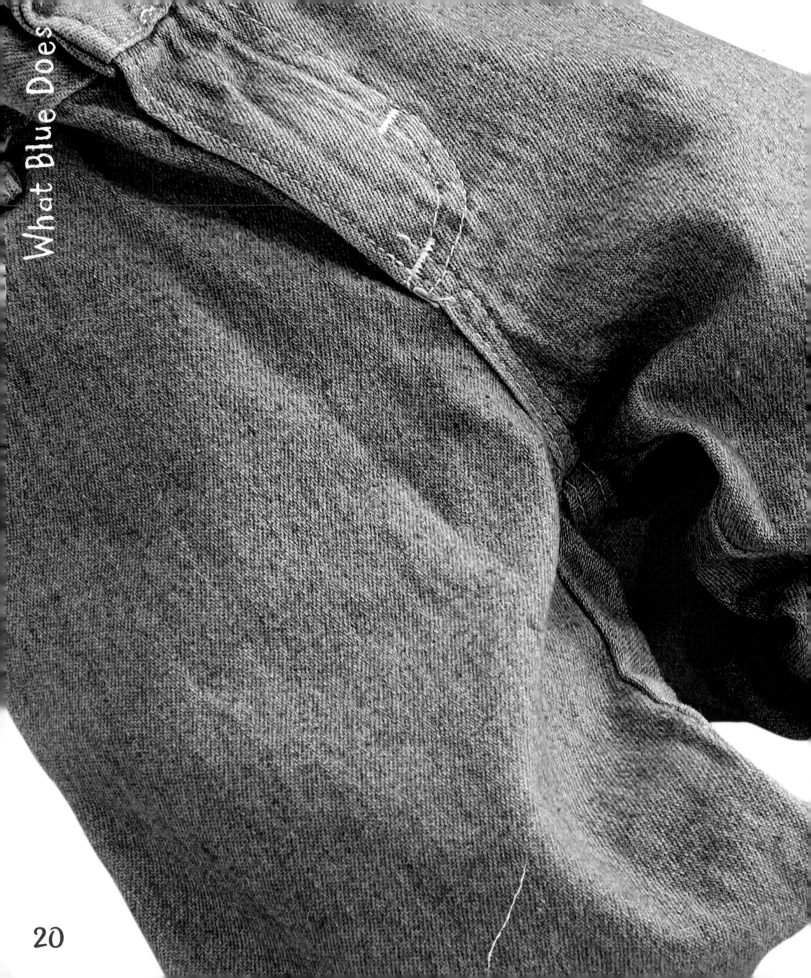

People all over the world wear blue denim shirts, jeans, and jackets. Blue denim is strong and lasts a long time.

Blue is strong.
Blue is warm.

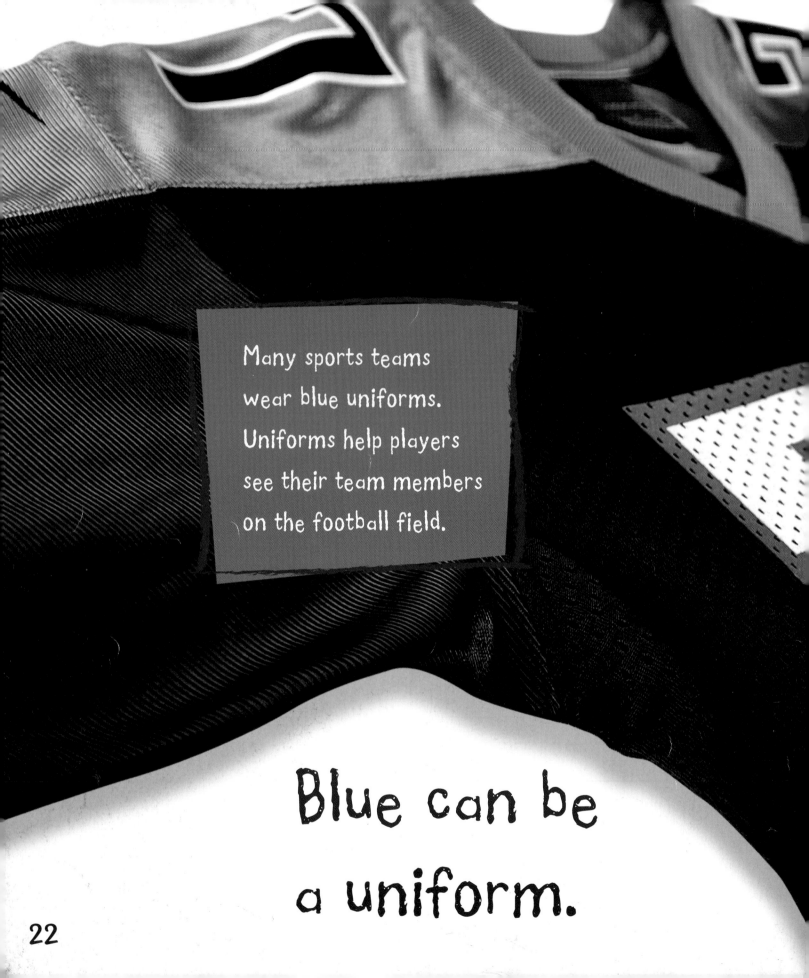

Many sports teams wear blue uniforms. Uniforms help players see their team members on the football field.

Blue can be a uniform.

Mail carriers pick up mail from blue mailboxes along city streets. They deliver mail around town.

Blue holds all our mail inside.

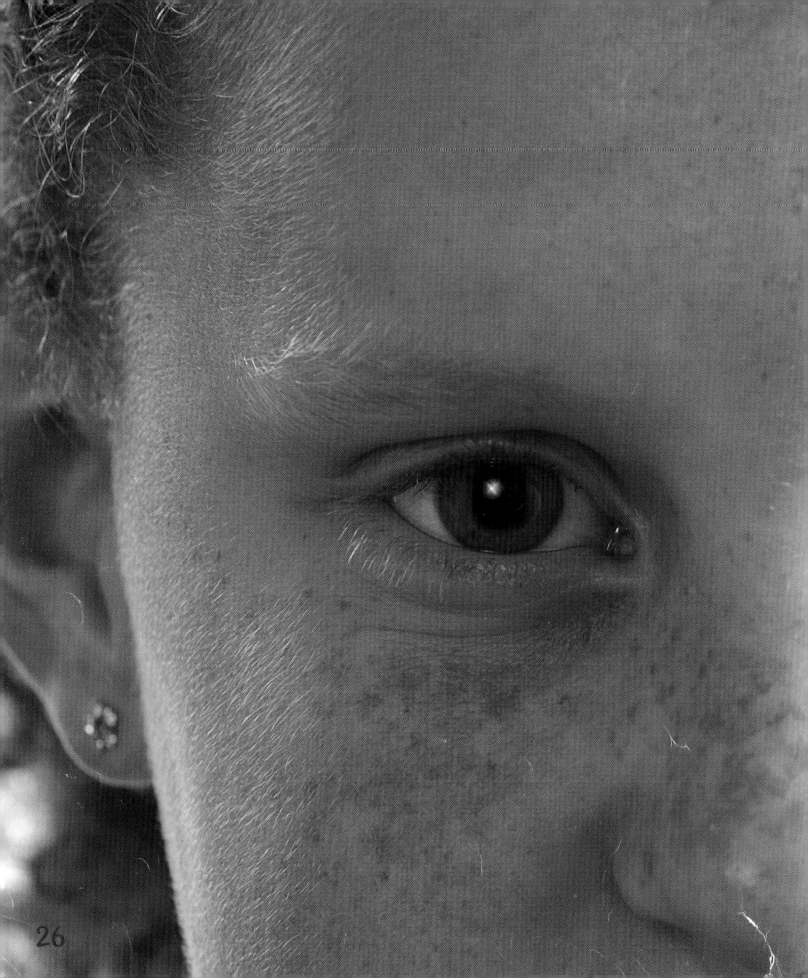

Blue can blink
and open wide!

Mixing Blue

Artists use a color wheel to know how to mix colors. Blue, red, and yellow are primary colors. They mix together to make secondary colors. Purple, orange, and green are the secondary colors they make. You can use blue to make green and purple.

color wheel

You will need

two pieces of paper

blue, red, and yellow finger paint

paper towel

1 Use your fingers to put a small amount of blue paint on one piece of paper. Then, wipe your fingers on a piece of paper towel.

2 Use your fingers to mix a small amount of yellow paint on top of the blue paint. What color do you make?

3 Repeat step 1 on the second piece of paper. Now, use your fingers to mix a small amount of red paint on top of the blue paint. What color do you make?

Words to Know

denim—a strong fabric made from cotton; denim usually is dyed blue.

feather—one of the light, fluffy parts that cover a bird's body; some birds have blue feathers.

fruit—the fleshy, juicy part of a plant that people eat

rain forest—a thick forest where rain falls almost every day

uniform—a set of clothing; members of a team usually wear uniforms; some workers wear uniforms at their jobs.

whale—a large ocean animal that looks like a fish; whales are mammals; they are warm blooded and feed milk to their young.

wingspan—the distance between the outer tips of a bird's wings; wingspan is usually measured when the wings are open.

Read More

Rea, Thelma. *I Wonder Why the Sky Is Blue.* Reading Room Collection. New York: Rosen, 2002.

Stone, Tanya Lee. *Living in a World of Blue.* Woodbridge, Conn.: Blackbirch Press, 2001.

Winne, Joanne. *Blue in My World.* The World of Color. New York: Children's Press, 2000.

Internet Sites

Blue PaintBear
http://www.thelittleartist.com/blue.html

Guess the Color
http://www.funbrain.com/color/index.html

I Love Colors—Blue
http://www.enchantedlearning.com/colors/blue.shtml

Index